STOCK CARS

by Lisa Bullard

Pull Ahead Books

Lerner Publications Company • Minneapolis

Here's a book for Michael and all his cars! —LB

This book is available in two editions:
Library binding by Lerner Publications Company, a division of Lerner Publishing Group
Soft cover by First Avenue Editions, an imprint of Lerner Publishing Group
241 First Avenue North
Minneapolis, MN 55401 U.S.A.

Website address: www.lernerbooks.com

Library of Congress Cataloging-in-Publication Data

Bullard, Lisa.
    Stock cars / by Lisa Bullard.
        p.   cm. – (Pull ahead books)
    Includes index.
    Summary: An introductory description of stock cars and stock car racing.
        ISBN: 0–8225–0694–7 (lib. bdg. : alk. paper)
        ISBN: 0–8225–9922–8 (pbk. : alk. paper)
        1. Stock cars (Automobiles)—Juvenile literature.
    2. Stock car racing—Juvenile literature. [1. Stock cars (Automobiles) 2. Stock car racing.] I. Title. II. Series.
    GV1029.9.S74B85 2004
    796.72–dc21   2003005625

Manufactured in the United States of America
1 2 3 4 5 6 – JR – 09 08 07 06 05 04

VROOOOOM! Stock cars roar.
The race is on!

Stock cars look like cars you see on the street. Do parts of this stock car look like other cars you have seen?

Some parts of a stock car, like the roof and the hood, are the same as a regular car.

But stock cars are special. They are built to win races.

The racing **engine** under the hood
powers a stock car.

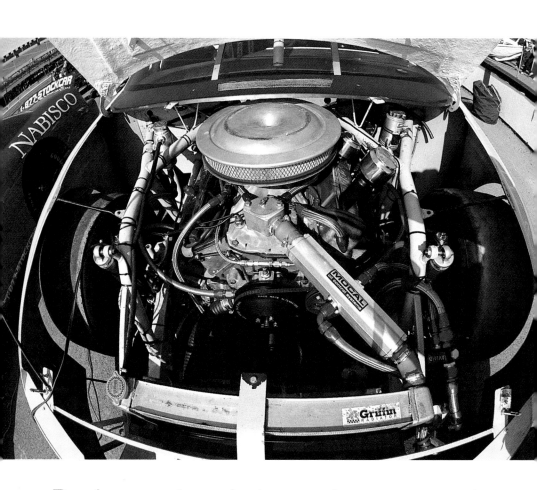

Racing engines help stock cars speed more than 200 miles per hour.

Stock cars need to cut through the air fast. But the air shouldn't slow down or lift up the car.

The **air dam** runs along the bottom front of the car. It blocks air from getting under the car and lifting it.

The rear spoiler stands up along the car's back end. It catches air. The air helps hold the car on the racetrack.

What's that sticking up from the roof? They are roof flaps. Roof flaps flip up to slow the car down. They help the driver control the car.

Sometimes stock cars crash. That's why stock cars are built to be safe.

The **frame** of a stock car is very strong. The driver is protected by a **roll cage** made of steel bars.

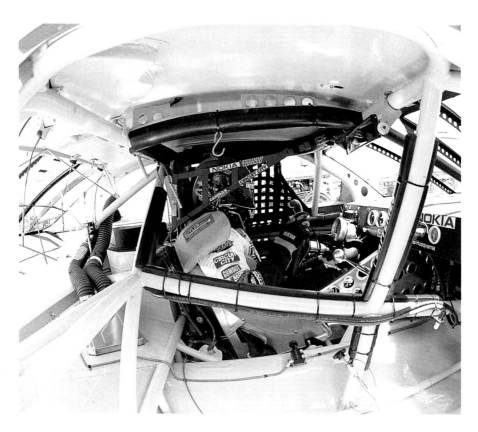

The driver has a type of seatbelt called a safety harness. The seat also protects the driver.

What is missing on the side of this car?

Stock cars have no doors! Drivers just
climb in and out.

A safety net hooks over the driver's window.

Where does the key go? Nowhere!
Drivers just flip a switch to start their cars.

There are gauges, or dials, on the **dashboard.** The gauges show the driver if the engine is working right.

What if something goes wrong during a race? The driver makes a **pit stop** in an area to the side of a racetrack.

Each car has its own pit crew. They fix the car. They also fill the fuel cell, or gas tank, in the back.

Sometimes the pit crew changes the tires. They can change all four tires faster than you can count to fifty.

Many stock cars race for NASCAR.
NASCAR is the National Association
for Stock Car Auto Racing. NASCAR
racing is popular in the United States.

Stock cars are covered in stickers with company names. The companies help pay for the cost of racing.

What do you get when you mix a speedy pit crew, a great driver, and the fastest stock car?

You get a winner! Then it's time to celebrate in **Victory Lane!**

Facts about Stock Cars

■ Stock cars don't have real glass headlights. They just have stickers where the headlights would be. Stock car windshields aren't glass either. They're plastic.

■ It gets very hot inside a stock car during a race. There's no air conditioning. So tubes blow cool air right into the driver's helmet!

■ Four types of cars compete in NASCAR's biggest races. They are the Ford Taurus, Chevrolet Monte Carlo, Pontiac Grand Prix, and Dodge Intrepid.

■ NASCAR also has races for stock trucks. They look like pickup trucks.

Parts of a Stock Car

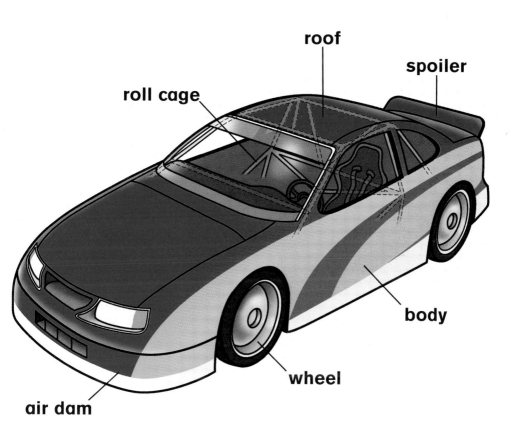

roof

spoiler

roll cage

body

wheel

air dam

Glossary

air dam: a part that runs along the bottom edge of the front of a stock car. It blocks air.

dashboard: the front inside of a car, where the steering wheel and gauges are

engine: the part of a stock car that gives it the power to move

frame: the part of a stock car that holds together the body, wheels, and engine

pit stop: a stop during a race in an area where a car can be fixed or gassed up

roll cage: a hard cage made of steel bars

Victory Lane: a special part of the track for the winner's celebration

Index

About the Author

Growing up, Lisa Bullard loved pretending to drive fast cars. She imagined that her bike, her brother's toy riding tractor, or even a kitchen chair was a speeding car. Now that she's a grown-up, she gets to write about race cars! She has also written nine other books for children, including *Powerboats* and the award-winning *Trick-or-Treat on Milton Street*. Lisa lives in Minneapolis, Minnesota, where she tries not to drive faster than the speed limit.

Photo Acknowledgments

The photographs in this book appear courtesy of: © Duomo/Corbis, pp. 3, 6; © Indianapolis Motor Speedway/Artemis Images, pp. 4, 5, 9, 21, 26, 27; ©ATD Group, Inc./Artemis Images, pp. 10,11; © Curtis Pilgreen Collection/Artemis Images, pp. 12, 15, 20, 22, 24; © Kevin Fleming/Corbis, pp. 7, 13, 16, 25; © Greg Crisp/SportsChrome East/West, pp. 8, 14; © Brian Spurlock/SportsChrome East/West, p. 18; © SportsChrome East/West, p. 19; © Alan Schein Photography/Corbis, p. 23; © Reuters NewMedia, Inc./CORBIS, pp. 17, 31. Illustration on p. 29 by Laura Westlund, © Lerner Publications Company. Front cover: © Craig Jones/Allsport by Getty Images.